# PEAL

# PEAL

poems by

## BRUCE

## BOND

etruscan press

Etruscan Press
Wilkes University
84 West South Street
Wilkes-Barre, PA 18766

 WILKES UNIVERSITY

www.etruscanpress.org

Printed in the United States of America

Publisher's Cataloging-in-Publication
(*Provided by Quality Books, Inc.*)

Bond, Bruce, 1954-
    Peal / Bruce Bond. -- 1st ed.
    p. cm.
    Poems.
    ISBN-13: 9780981968704
    ISBN-10: 0981968708

    I. Title.

    PS3552.O5943P43 2009        811'.54
                        QBI09-600127

First Edition

Design by Michael Ress

Etruscan Press is committed to sustainability and environmental steward-
ship. We elected to print this title through Bookmobile on FSC paper that
contains 30% post consumer fiber manufactured using biogas energy and
100% wind power.

# Acknowledgments

The author would like to thank the editors of the following journals in which these poems first appeared:

| | |
|---|---|
| *Agni* | "The Last Days of Jaco Pastorius" |
| *Boston Review* | "Elegy" |
| *Boulevard* | "Górecki" |
| *The Cincinnati Review* | "Estate" |
| *Colorado Review* | "Elegy for Tim Buckley" |
| *Crab Orchard Review* | "Homage to Georges Bizet" |
| | "Scar" |
| *Elixir* | "Djembe" |
| | "White" |
| *The Georgia Review* | "A Diet of Angels" |
| *Harvard Review* | "Confessions of a Music Box" |
| *Image* | "Elysium" |
| | "The Human Share" |
| *The Iowa Review* | "Madam Zero" |
| *Measure* | "Lark Ascending" |
| *The New Republic* | "The Invention of Song" |
| *Ploughshares* | "Ringtone" |
| *Poetry Northwest* | "Rock" |
| *Prairie Schooner* | "Abyss of Birds" |
| | "The Burning Boy" |
| *Provincetown Arts* | "Morning Elegy" |
| *Raritan* | "A Boy in the Thicket" |
| *River Styx* | "Two Dreams with a Brief Waking in the Middle" |
| *Sewanee Review* | "Death Mask" |
| *Subtropics* | "Tuning Fork" |
| *Third Coast* | "Peal" |
| *Virginia Quarterly Review* | "Ash" |
| *Western Humanities Review* | "Homage to the Ear" |
| *The Yale Review* | "Body and Soul" |

"Ringtone" appeared in *Best American Poetry 2009* (Scribner's) and "Two Dreams with a Brief Waking in the Middle" also appeared in the London journal *Naked Lunch*. "Ash" was republished in *Poetry Calendar 2008* (Alhambra Press, Belgium). "Elegy for Tim Buckley," "Scar," "Tuning Fork," and "Confessions of a Music Box" were featured by *Verse Daily*. In addition, the author would like to thank Nicki Cohen, Corey Marks, and John Tait for their time and wisdom during the completion of this manuscript.

# Contents

# Górecki

The slowly sweeping wheel of dust and iron
is not the upended carriage with no place
to go or call its home. Clearly we are somewhere
just to the south of something so embodied,
let us call it home. Let us call it a city
pocked with the aftermath of too many nights
to make a passage of, too many rattled
windows to settle in their grooves, however
washed in the sweets of lilacs and small street fires,
the occasional waft from the morning bakery.
It's here where the arc of the symphony
begins, out of the black bricks of Warsaw,
the gradual rise an enormous brood, the bass
viols, heavy, yes, though no less bowed,
glacial as a passage in a difficult book,
a book full of breath and the light it stretches
to extinction, a book you press to your chest
to feel the heat of your body slowly melt
the jacket and its pages, a book passing
into winds to lift you out of bed, to rake
the vagrant leaves across your roof. A winter
breezes through the large and hollow gate,
through the arc that is the shape a stone throws,
an all too sluggish siren bearing the heart
on its gurney, rising and falling, rising and falling.
A sun crowns the statuary horizon,
above the organ feet that walk up the dark

into the gabled room of belated song.
Always another ambulance to trail
the long and diminishing thread of hope
into ruin. And as we lie in bed,
we follow it, and what it follows. Even
the sigh of not knowing would have us
go on, the weary quietude that falls
to hypnotize the great symphonic wheel.
Even the part in the music where the flames
subside, the chapel in a spirit cloud
of smoke and rosin. Even the body's
diminuendo, the fading breath that waking
brings, the slowing pulse. First the bodies,
then the names: that's the way it is
with history. The sheer numbers darken
heaven's page. The red iron of a city's
carriage spins in the air. Part of the power
of what we hear is the sense we revisit
a place we never knew. Moved, we say.
In the way of blood, air, hand, stomach, eye.
As if even the respite of song is action,
its silence no less. Even the bend and reach
of architecture that rises out of the smolder
and back, even the legs of the arc that return
the way the sun returns to a black well,
its trespass quiet, slow, a ghost, a coin,
a wish gone deep as the day grows old.

# Body and Soul

Where to find a cab in the morning dark;
where a phone booth doused in rain, in light;
what to make of these nights and the wreck
they lift out of the body, out of a slit

in the known world, to sink again each dawn.
To lift, the way the saxophonist lifts
the head of his exhausted tune, the lantern
in his bronze hands giving off what life

it will. He cannot count the times now
he played this ballad, this *Body and Soul*,
all the love-drunk versions he made new
and not new, the borrowed air that spilled

through nameless hands before him, that passed
out over smoldering laughter in a place
like this, over the clink of soiled glass
again and again. More than knowing this piece

by heart, this home key drifting up one step
to lead him burning to the bridge and back.
More than the weary man who will not sleep,
who cracks open his heart like a fake-book

to read the barest measures of the past.
There will always be a dim lounge, a corner
in this waste of dishes, where the soloist
seals his eyes, expanding. Always a minor

liberty startled by the sound it makes.
He breathes a bit, takes the lip of his horn
out of his mouth, to clear a quiet space
for the brush and cymbal, who yield in turn

a deeper quiet. And the upright bass bends
softly now, though bold in what it asks
of silence. And in the stillness of the hand
that listens, a last smoke clinging to its ash.

## Abyss of Birds
*for Ann*

What it must be to watch the music
fade out of your fingers, your clarinet
slipped into the felt of its casket
like a child's puzzle, the small-
winged hinges of its valves grown
stubborn, stiff. Call it the swell
of something foreign in the hand,
or rather the foreigner that is
the hand. The black flower of the bell,
the long red scar of a surgeon's
cut, what are they now against
the inevitable. Once a nurse
told you to go ahead and practice
the piece you most love. Strangely,
a *Quartet for the End of Time.*
She could not know just how far
the reach. Still you hear the birds there
in your stillness, how they rise
like ashes. You hear the composer's
*abyss,* as he put it, locked inside
his stalag where his notes took the shape
of an angel's sword. *No more,*
says the sword, the sweep, the prisoner's
faith. You have no such faith.
The body moves its way and you
move with it. But with these birds,

7

the way you listen, with the sharpness
of the instrument, its voice continues
to defy a language. Not unlike
the origin of language. Somewhere
your hand stiffens about a pen.
You listen for the slice of the wing,
the wind surprising a reed, how,
like music, you never quite arrive.
You could lose yourself for hours.
That's the odd mercy, you say,
the difficulty of the comfort here.
Like silence after a piece you love
when, however clear the mind,
it is impossible to know
where music ends, the world begins.

## The Invention of Song

Not the face, the human face,
floating in its crippled spoon;
not the needle where it drinks
night after night; neither the watch,
the blood, nor the gold in hock,
the world liquified to small bills
passed under the broker's jail;
no little crime of sweat that breaks
the child's lockbox of the body;
not the courage of the dour road
where it blisters into rough stone;
or the craze of the eye regarding
itself, the obsidian crystal;
not the mockery of the beast lung
bursting through its two blue doors;
or the shriek of birds glorified
with fear; not the pitch, the rock,
the ship of deaf sailors save one
lashed to his mast; not even the gash
of stars, the song, we are told,
too sweet to bear; but something
more, always more, the moon
in the wave, the animal, they say,
running in the Siren's veins,
the squall in the breach that calls
him out, mast or no mast, that grips
the buried shield of the sternum

as if it were the world's shield,
as if the heart dropped its massive
rope to hear, there, drowned in fog,
the sudden distance of its name.

# Elegy

Once I swore grief was the same distance
from lament as joy from praise, the same
that stretched a pillow's wing at night, a space
I'd never close completely, I'd never lose.

You know the feeling, I'm sure: the hymn
that tends the fire inside it, that keeps it safe.
But if songs are bridges to a world in flames,
don't bridges too catch fire. I want to believe

there is more pleasure in songs of loss
than loss in any song that pleases. But then
who could lose oneself inside a song
that never dies. One day our grieving turns

to lament the way a widow turns to her
remaining child. Is happiness any less
the widow, any less the mother who sees
herself in the one she prays she won't

survive. One day a mother's elegy turns
back to joy to say, don't I know you.
Another life, perhaps. Another sun
burns its arc in the slow zero of praise

we live inside, the one that lives, keeping
its vital distance. Perhaps we see praise
in the inconsolable eyes of the living.
Seeing itself is distance. And what is praise

without seeing. What are songs without
a shape that silence gives them. See that cat
who knows less of praise than the joy
that knows no joy. I love that cat. See

the birds who, or so the songs imagine,
lament our laments, though we know
better, seeing and not seeing. Like nothing
the zeroes of these eyes, these wings.

# Confessions of a Music Box

No larger than a bird coffin,
the kind that opens its one wing
onto a sky it cannot take to,

save as the thin and silver trickle
of a tune, a feather fanning
the ghost goodbye, as if to say, yes,

it's true, how the ancients saw it,
that music is the sound numbers
make on the verge of extinction

or sleep, whatever comes first,
that it sends its arrows through
the ear's window, clean through and yet

attached, brightening the glass.
That's why a monk I read loved
music, not merely for the holy

signatures, the geometry
of tones that are its body, but how
that body dies again and again,

how it slips its box like steam, like gold.
Ask any star in the Greek
toy chest of stars, any sphere,

and it returns you to an image
of this, to the singing of a thing
you wind, or someone winds, the grind

of a song it never tires of.
A lullaby. How like a box
to hoard its measure of nothing

we speak of until, that is, the box
of dark inside breaks, confessing
the way an old grief confesses

or some nocturnal heating vent
pouring air between its teeth.
But then…if you call this news,

it is never news enough.
Only paired phrases like a doll
house on fire, like the small

murmur of a child at her bed,
talking to a god she has only
heard of, a father locked up in

the rhymes of parables, of hymns:
*and if I die before I wake.*
Either way she dies, she wakes.

# Tuning Fork

Lynchpin of the singing wheel,
  you with the silver of your call
  so tiny and, yes, unmusical

at times, your shiny monotone
  a mere shiver down the spine
  of the steel, the nerve, the wine

glass so quick to speak, to startle
  at your touch, its hollow bell
  overflowing with the chill

that silence drinks. As does the shape
  of seasoned violins who sleep
  beside you in their cases, who slip

at night from some determined pitch
  and form of things. *True*, we call it,
  as in *true north*, winter's pivot

we steer below, what we balance
  in the heaven of our compass.
  *True*, the way the rifle in us

aims to see, to make true the cross
  that sees. *True*, as in the thrust
  of birth, or death, the things we trust

to be there when we draw the curtain.
        Is there nothing under the sun
        more sure, more fragile than your song.

Of all the birds the hummingbird.
        You who hover with the speed
        of the atom, the blur of being

here alive. It's what you hear
        passed as one symphonic rumor
        from string to string, ear to ear,

through the sea of all the sour
        fiddling, our uncertain water
        from which a music crawls ashore.

Straight as light itself—the sound
        you make—as the shaft we send
        flying from the bow of sight.

Not much of a song really.
        Not yet. More of a tune we bury
        in bodies of the tunes we play,

a perfect thing (and so not
        a thing at all) our one clear note
        deep inside the rippling planet.

# Ringtone

As they loaded the dead onto the gurneys
to wheel them from the university halls,
who could have predicted the startled chirping
in those pockets, the invisible bells
and tiny metal music of the phones,
in each the cheer of a voiceless song.
Pop mostly, Timberlake, Shakira, tunes
never more various now, more young,
shibboleths of what a student hears,
what chimes the dark doorway to the parent
on the line. Who could have answered there
in proxy for the dead, received the panic
with grace, however artless, a live bird
gone still at the meeting of the strangers.

# Death Mask

And when a panic in them stilled the hand
that reached to shroud the head of the composer,
the living few who remained summoned

the maker of the casts to lay a plaster
over the deep sleep and bell-shape of his face,
his small face made smooth again, his pallor

drained of character, of thunder and stress.
*The immortal beloved*—that too died,
the secret of his dedication we take less

to heart than to a grave, where his ode
sang something universal, laid its bloom,
and walked away. That his tempers grew old,

without question. That love escaped him,
so they say. That some unfinished piece
vanished from his desk that night, some hymn

to night, quiet as the hand that pours
the mask, that seals the chamber of the eye,
the mouth, the passage of each hollow place.

Take this look so like his there's thievery
in it, as in any romantic gaze we love
to the point of extinction, any body

that turns into music and so dissolves.
*The immortal beloved*—whoever it was
(if ever who) whatever love survives

in time to raise a peroration, what waves
the fire of signatures across the surface
of the score, one thing is certain: it weaves

a contrary motion with its voices.
It lives, it dies. Why else this descending
height as the bass moves up, this fist

that closes with its counterpoint, that ends
in music's shadowbox, a phantom bread.
If not matter, then freely a dependence,

a throw of birds above a lake, reflected.
The maker of casts lifts the plaster mold
which in turn will spawn a brotherhood

of masks, some as curios, some models
for the sculptor, fetishes of grief
however distant, some as histories made

to take us back, but more than this, to give
loss a face, to send our fortunes forward.
That it was there, and will be, like a grave

about the literal man: a fact no word
can touch. Only touch itself, the greed
of touch's privacy. And yes, absurd.

As if to hold the tree inside the gourd,
the breath in the vowel, the hymn beneath
the polish of his silence. Sure, we guard

a body in the end knowing it worthless,
lower a corpse with the shy decorum
that frames a song we admire. The wraith

of skin is for part of us neither dead
nor alive, not wholly, like the nerves
of strings inside a harp. The darkly clustered

chord you play, to play it twice is never
as dissonant. The dead too have ears
fading from the bone the way a composer

fades into the deafness of his final years.
It's then, we learn, he will write his most
mortal passages. Joy. Not the mere

facsimile but the embodiment
of joy, something poured over the heads
of those in the choir. Something to meet

each face, to say it was there, once, behind
the dead, ahead of the living. Somewhere
a boy leans toward a giant speaker, the hidden

pulsing of its O. Somewhere he hears
the melodies braid into one another,
the anticipated beat before the measure

tumbling into stride. He is leaning closer
stormed by grace. He is letting the cloudburst
go right through him, straight through. And will not stir.

II

# Morning Elegy

When I wake, I am restored, alone.
Each day in the bones of my face
I feel my father's face emerging.

I look for quiet openings, signs:
an inheritance of shirts, a marble Lincoln
on the table, how the grass exhales

the aging scent of rain. But they take me
only so far before the road bends
the way a nurse's language bends

to let me down with uneasy mercy.
Today, I tell myself, is a good day.
The year returns me like a heavy book.

Outside, the wind in the leaves
turning and falling, turning and falling.
The morning elms reclaim their shadows.

It frightens me, how we lean into the world
the way the largest of the bells leans
in its only tower. Six o'clock.

My mother calls me by my father's name.
The judicial eyes in his photo gaze
always at the air behind me, ever vigilant,

ever still. Who wouldn't want to break
the man, to melt the silent window
of his trance. And then I remember,

the other father, stitching the vines
of tomatoes in their spidery cages,
how I caught him once looking down

in disbelief—or so I see it—at his feet
the drowsy flash of minnow rising,
eating the mirrored remnants of the sky.

# Ash

And so I handed over my father's box
of ashes, its odd white weight, the brick
of a life compacted there as if it gripped
the man inside it. Unsteady as a rock,

the way it wavered in the hole it entered
slowly, blindly, dipped into the balm
of shadow, the ashes' last descending gesture
like a boy releasing his baffled palms.

Then it seemed to draw us in, to the wet
eye of broken earth that held us, gathered
closer, newly fathered by the quiet,
morning made strange by the cloud cover

of what we wore, by a mist that woke
out of the ground. Soon it was everywhere:
the exhalation of a night that walked
so long, so far, to stagger into the fire

of day, into the world inside the flame.
It was ours, this world, its dying wind
like a name set down in a field of names,
too heavy now to carry in our hands.

# The Burning Boy
## *after Freud*

Begin with a father, exhausted
by the long night watch at the bedside
of his child. When the boy dies,
the man retires to the next room,
door ajar, and goes to sleep
leaving behind the child's bed
fringed in candles, in the words
of an older man who murmurs
something to God or the boy,
difficult to tell, something soft
so as not to wake the child,
not yet, or to wake him and not
at the same time. Think of prayer
as an answer, the kind that ends
in a question, looking up
to shudder the flame on its wick.
It's a story with no known
source, for all we know a fable,
mysterious as money changing
hands, as the visions we spend
our nights retelling, sleeping the sleep
of strangers, blowing the coals.
Soon the old man too drifts off,
and the father dreams the boy
comes back to life, that he stands
overhead, clasps the father's arm,

and says: *Don't you see, don't you see*
*I am burning.* You can guess
the rest: how the father wakes
to something brightening the door,
the old man asleep, the child's
arm burned by a fallen candle.
You can guess the reasons why.
Say the father, as he slept, saw
the neighboring light, the literal.
Say he recalled a day the boy
looked up in a fever and said
those same words. Possible.
What a father doesn't know hurts,
true. And yet a certain comfort
flickers in the mouths of doors.
It too wants to live, to preserve
its blindness beside him as he sleeps.
If he had slept any longer,
who knows. But a near disaster
gave the boy a second wind,
if only briefly, a reason to move
farther into the father's mind:
a savior come back to save himself
who is past saving, past needing
to be saved. And the father knew this,
or his dream at least, when it opened
its eye on the boy's returning
gesture. *Don't you see, don't you,*
as if suffering begets suffering

to bring a child closer. To remember
by forgetting, defying the end
of the story, the moment the boy
becomes two bodies, two lives lost
deep inside a father's, to lift
him from his sleep like smoke.

# Two Dreams with a Brief Waking in the Middle

And I saw my mother as she was before,
shivering, alive, gilded by our fire
in the woods, come to break her history
like bread, for now it was my turn to see
her through—healthy as she was I knew
the greater story, both of us knew—now
my turn to puzzle out the ruined language
of the dying, while all about me the foliage
exhaled its summer flies down the rock path
to the Susquehanna. At dusk the earth
released a craze of bats above the water
where the fish too rose in their hunger,
striking air. Illegible, the never
repeating cursive, the speed of the river
nicked with stars, the stationary stars.

Then I was walking into town and heard
familiar voices: a feast with a large bird
at the center, a childhood friend igniting
with hello. But the others like the night
remained aloof, cold even, and I pulled
away. Which is when my friend explained
the old among us had all decided to die,
and I took the black wine of that idea
to my mother who said gently it's true:
she decided as well. And the blue
in her eye dissolved until she was all

pupil, entering mine. I too dissolved
inconsolable, though strangely held
like a cloud dragged over the night
it dims, hemmed only in the sparks behind it.

# Rock

You who will not, cannot burn,
on every side the fire returned
to grit, smoke, to something less
than smoke, to the fallen place
of every man who cannot put
his mind to rest, who pries apart
the kindling of his sleep, its river
of heat flown over and over.
You who hide beneath the spit
and grapple of the flame, the pit
lit up with inarticulate
grief, with the self-consuming light
of speech. You a child the world
leaves its losses; its final will,
as the living say, executed.
Of all things you, once created
out of fire, now an exile
in its midst, beneath the trickle
of rising sparks, as if the blaze
had gone on ahead, raised
like some blind gesture of faith.
What is it that you unearth,
what brief incarnations of fever,
of doubt, of fable, whatever
bewilders the boy as he stares
at the crux of the campfire's
constant turning. What do you bring

to light, you who never sing
beneath the kettle, whose silence
seems so crystalline, so tense.
What jewels glimmer in your coffin.
One boy watches embers soften
sinking in their bone-white skin
and gives in to his exhaustion.
Fire closes its door of soot.
One boy dreams of you, a slate
the fury washes to a black.
In the morning ash beneath his stick
it's you he finds, like a knowledge
he cannot know, a boundary, a bridge,
a thing he calls *dead*, for want
of a more transparent word.
You too are beyond your reach.
Everything you cipher you touch.
You, we say, beyond the taint
of fire, though the one thing faintly
warm still, like an afterlife,
a distant blaze, the kind that lies
down, having lagged so far behind,
darkly burning in a child's hand.

# A Boy in the Thicket

And when he comes to the edge of the park
where veins of ivy camouflage the foot
of some forgotten path, where they fret
the oaks in hopeless tangles, he brushes apart

a rustled veil of flies, opens the web
of tendrils falling there, netting his face.
And then the sluggish rain of the place:
the glaze of worms descending on their threads,

dropped from nothing into the visible,
into the unlikely sense of memory
before memory, or long after maybe:
the shoe, the can, a wasp as it sizzles

in the sweet stale dark. And in the sky—
or what was once a sky—a puzzle of trees,
the living ink that stains the backs of leaves
in tiny shatter patterns like an eye.

Still he wanders eye to eye to handpick
the lock of the briars, wincing as it cuts,
blazing a trail with the legs that takes it.
Which is when it comes, the broken fabric

of a squirrel wreathed in black, a mound
of scavengers pouring through its ear,
running in rivulets over the stiff fur.
Grain by grain they bear each morsel down

into the maze, into the thing that spoils,
he thinks, the very ground he is kneeling
over, all this time entranced, unknowing.
It's what he later pictures, as he pulls

a blanket over his eyes to sleep, to lose
the world, yes, and yet to make it over,
to lose himself, like the woods a man remembers
faintly, ever stranger to the boy he was.

# Scar

What is it you forget in your vigil,
cell after cell like petals on the grave
of first days, so often strange, your veil
of skin ruffled, renewed, as if you grieved

in the blind color of too much light.
So late you sleep there, so leaden the pour
of suns that cannot touch you. The blood you let,
the foaming of the crevice—what old prayer

of needle and thread could ever answer
the power of arrival. The body opens
its red door which in turn opens the flare
of the eye. Don't you remember. You pinned

each to itself like an armless sleeve.
Unlikely, true. White shadow of the wound
that is no wound. The wind in the leaves
and the sound it makes, after the wind.

# Madam Zero

Who can say what the silence said
to Madam Zero—that's what the other
patients called her—*I am dead,*
she claimed, *and yet I live forever.*

*Live,* the way a fugitive lives
in a strange land, the mother tongue
a childhood music that leaves
a little more each night, each dawn.

And what could touch her, I ask,
she who lay like black on black
water, what pried her from the lake
of her bed, peeled her like a mask.

She saw her image everywhere
as the thing that was missing,
the quartz in the stone, the sleeper's stare,
the clock's dice clicking in its fist.

She was the hunger of the cloud
that breaks on the darkened ocean,
the surge that cannot be consoled,
that cannot slip the shore it's in.

Doubtless I too would have shied
away, glanced down at my breakfast
in fear, in shame. Who am I
to cross her, to wake a night like this.

And yet, here, tonight, as I think
of a mother in her madness
alone, how she hovers on the brink
of no place, it's true, how Madam

Zero put it, that the living die
into a life where it's hard for us
to call them, where the long dry
valley gathers up its branches,

where the mother studies a bedside
photo slow to name the faces
looking back, each bright figure iced
where it stands in a still glaze

of unremembered joy: a slice,
if you will, beyond death's peace
or the smoke of breathing, pressed
beneath the heaven of the glass.

# The Human Share

For He so loved the world, goes the book,
as if in dying He died our death, crossing
over, not simply into heaven and back,
but into each particular heaven, the icons

of its lakes so like ours, like a mirror
that drinks the lightened fog of breathing,
so that this solitude we learn to bear
keeps slipping forward, terrified as birth,

slipping the way a record needle slips
holding still, or the lover who leans
with closed eyes, or even as we sleep
the endless voice of a distant ocean,

a shush of waves, how they come to rest
again and again, as if we too were
ever departing, arriving, ever the breath
no friend takes for us, taking it away.

# Elysium

But most dangerous of all is the dream
of the Elysian fields, the casting pool
by the cliffs of the arroyo, a serum
of clouds above and below, as if you,

like the cloud, were made oblivious:
a drizzle of hooks severing the mirror.
You cannot view what the chokecherry views,
the bare tuber that digs beneath the mire.

To never fear what fear invokes: this day
polished with a homeland's foreign water.
Most dangerous of all is the body
that is no body, emptied of the clutter,

of the veins that arm the briar, the rose.
Like hope. Your heart the size of your two fists.
Who crosses your path once you have closed
that gate; what barbed root, what writhing fish.

# A Diet of Angels

So little to go on. The blade in the fan,
the warm sour air, my mother's limbs light
as a puppet in our arms. So few signs

but the vital ones, the final measures
of morphine and oxygen—*a diet of angels,*
we say, laughing oddly, softly, careful

with our grief as though it were sleeping.
To see her damaged look of awe, that look
of singing to someone in the distance

grown small, her voice erased in the labor
of her breathing. No more, say the leaves.
No life to waste on the gathering of life.

Then her eyes open thinly in the half dark,
and I fit her glasses over the sunken hazel,
those twin wells glazed in the last of her

body's water. Never so starless, so still.
I hold my head above them like a lamp.
The next life. What can I say of things

that frighten speech into hope or hiding.
What news do I bring to the open mouth.
She moans a bit, and we check the clock.

Soon. The crystal of her next narcotic.
Soon the dropper and its pinch of seed
so quick to flower, bitter under the tongue.

The smaller she gets, the stronger the temple
welling up with inaudible music.
Just yesterday she was calling to the dead.

*Who's there*, she said, *Who*—the faint survival
of her fluster going soft, mute, leading her
to a door at her bedside, the door that was not there.

All homes are her home. The one she left.
And now the shrinking of the room inside
the room. *Be well*, I say, my hand in the white

fire of her hair. Somewhere is a word
to bury the words between us. Somewhere near.
And the map of the world looks on, rough

with wear, its scattering of bright pins
for the cities she's been to, their tiny names
flowing into harbors. Each continent

is an island here. Each view a god's.
Each ship invisible. And a blue, the fallen
color of the sky, to keep the shores apart.

Estate

And now the ledger, the blade,
the greed of grief dividing up
its last effects: a child's bed,
a host of lanterns, a broken clock
ferried down from hand to hand.

If you wait long, it tells time:
*never, always, never, always.*
A miniature cathedral, this clock,
the stiffened midnight of its steeple.
And we the children of the hour.

We unwrap china from the clouds
of tissue paper, speaking softly.
So slender, the wings of the handles,
light as the names we're given,
box after box of bones and sky.

Suddenly it's one great sad Christmas,
the kind that visits only once,
where the world is ours to drag
home, to hold, to hold us, to take
us in. We could stare for ages.

Tomorrow is an ancient painting
of snow that will not fall, not quite,
a house made of ice on the backs
of our eyes. Go on, we tell the world,
be better than us, go prosper, live.

III

# Homage to the Ear

Before words, before hunger took the shape
of words, the many shapes of chaos inside
the language of the others; before the slap

that broke us when first we spit the world
to clear our lungs, you were in there somewhere.
You were the eye to lead the eye that hid

in ways you couldn't, save inside the core
of sleep, your only silence. Though even then
you were the one dim lamp in the corner

of our house, far from the dark distraction
that consumed us. And now, look at you.
Harp of the Flesh, the way you take us down

the underworld of what we cannot know.
With every music another corridor
not unlike your own, your passage through

the body to the tiny bone of the stirrup
that goads us, wakes us; to the small hammer
that animates its anvil with a whisper.

And beyond that the water creature
of the deepest regions, our labyrinth
to keep our balance, our xylophone of hair

inside the cochlea that curls its length
into a tight spin, a final question.
Go ahead and ask. Hear the quiet strength

of your language rising, its curved song
of uncertainty, the swing of its door.
Or the way beneath our hands the ocean

in you seems to draw a little closer.
The more still we are the stronger the hush
that falls, that breaks against the warm enclosure.

Our first sound, you like to think, this wash
of air going through, though in the womb
it was your mother's breath, and you the fish

beneath the tide. Who were you to come
into this strange land you could not know
as strange, to listen locked inside the tomb

of life. What was once a mother's breath grows
into your own, more alien now than ever.
You are the rumpled sail of a ship that goes

nowhere, that lies deep inside its harbor,
awaiting the lure of some gulf stream
drawn beneath the keel, some wind to bear

you out of solitude, a constant drum
of blood, of surf, to take you from the cove
that is yours alone, and give the wind a name.

# Homage to Georges Bizet

It started with his tongue, his throat,
the inflammation that flared up
from time to time; all his life
the spells, the fever, as if unfinished

music blew the embers in him,
flew them through the path of drink,
of song. *It started with his throat,*
history says, knowing so little

where death begins, if it's the sound
he conceived gazing in the Seine,
the melody that followed him
though the maze of soiled streets,

in and out of moods that fell
like shadows from the high walls.
In the end he swore the Paris air
had poisoned him. In his head

the two bold notes of ground bass
dragged from one ear to another,
forever dragging, as if to carve
a darker path against the dark.

All night the thrum of the chamber,
the fray of the bow. It was the best
he could do, his *Carmen*, and yet
not all he expected, not quite

the slash and burn of another spring.
Still he threw its Spanish aria
like a flower into the chest of his
last day. He too was a Carmen.

He loved both bull and the brute
that killed him, the flare of the song
with such duress, such light to shed.
There's power in the absurd

violence raised to an art,
in the eye of the lover who stares
you in the face and says, *I want,*
*I want.* Though more than this: *I am.*

The love-sick corporal in the drama—
who was he but the animal
he knew so little and so became.
In the end the two bold notes

dragged through Bizet like a fighter
and his dead bull, until the one ear,
the first, went weary, deaf. Yes,
the animal always dies offstage.

But something of the fanfare—
the dancers, picadors, bandilleros—
spilled into footlights, horrified
that such a soldier went so far

he had one ear in the other
world already. No less a beast,
bowed, furious, castrated, armed.
And then the final absurdity.

How fortunate. For those who stay
what more could they want: that leap
of disbelief, the moment the man
plunges his dagger in, plunges

the strong dark chord—call it the will
to die, to live, to die by living—
and with it the signature dissonance
of the one who cannot love him back—

cannot, will not—the same cold notes
that follow her everywhere,
even as she buckles over the blade
and the song's blood comes streaming out.

# Lark Ascending
*for Helen*

Why is it her most cautious years
bring this tendril, this curl, this ear
for the vines of music inside
the music, the waterfall design
of cellos that irrigate the woods
in *The Lark Ascending*. Winds
rustle through the lower voices
as in turn the solo violin's
flits above the clusters: a piece
her memory of hands repeats
faintly, shyly, dropping feathers.
So why is it now, her fingers
knotted like mended rope, why
this largesse beneath the sky's
cloud and variations: *face
the music*, says the child who plays
the executioner, his crosshairs
like a bowed string frozen there
for the final wish. How is it
an ancient body goes farthest
into spring's foliage as it cuts.
The wings of the f-holes sculpt
the ghost, calling the way one bird
calls out to another, the unheard
lark so long expected we take it
for lost, for some forsaken part

of us, some counterpointing wound.
She hears it echo in the sounds
of April, in the stems of bass
violins shivering the stage.
She follows in the way the closing
measures follow, into the slow
gathering of the cadenza
broken from the trees, a cappella,
over the cadence where it trills
like a flame on a wick, until
a silence, and the quiet that lifts
a vague chord, a thing so soft
she leans into its horizon,
holds her breath to feel it rise.

# The Last Days of Jaco Pastorius

Go back and hear *Three Views of a Secret*,
its little Florida of fog and whisper,
how the man inside it lies there, listening,

and underneath his bed a bass guitar,
a voice to pull the weather to the earth,
to root each chord in the netherworld

of chords—tough to resist, the gravity
of the open *E*, popped and ringing,
how it tugs the hem of sky's blue fabric

like a child. And a bold one at that.
Not merely the descent, the punch of smoke,
the dilated eye of the largest speaker.

There's authority to a note's decay,
to the shaded bell-tones rocking in their tower.
Each an elegy to the one before.

*The world's greatest,* he said, and they believed
to hear him wing it over a page of changes
as if there were wind in his instrument.

So easy to take the ground for granted,
to ignore the bones inside the body,
the solo idiom of nocturnal birds.

It was he who saw the future there,
who shamelessly plied the nickel frets
from the rosewood of a bass he borrowed.

Surely the soil had opened its box of bees.
Anything for the pitch of the moment,
for that liberal feel along the fingerboard,

the bead of his callus gliding on its string.
You would think his bass had swallowed someone,
and it had, the way a language wavered

in its throat, or an almost language, a moan
at times, there where loss begins to take
shape, to crown as something foreign, new.

Somehow that seemed closest to the life
to come, the one that grew small inside
the epithet, inside the legend, the god,

the lie that gripped him like a last coin.
If his myth gave way, it broke the way
a seal breaks on a fifth of Black Label.

Another draught to chase his lost sons,
lost wings, his stolen Fender, the days he lost
in the halls of Bellevue, stepping slow

to his *Thorazine Waltz.* Once he drummed
a solo on the coffin of a friend.
Death walked homelessly close beside him

those final nights sleeping on the b-ball
courts, the beaten leather in his arms.
Or throwing curses in the eyes of strangers.

Death was one such stranger, looking back
through the troubled gaze of a priest, a fan,
or the angry bouncer who took him down.

No accounting for the hope that suddenly
turned for the worse, the dream he would emerge
from the silence of his coma, an Orpheus

ascending the fretted ladder. Even then
as they pulled the plug and his breath went
still, his heart kept on. Three hours it beat

alone, going down the shaft, searching
for signs of life, of air, for a bird
cage among the rubble, a flutter of ash.

# Elegy for Tim Buckley

*In the streets we walk as beggars*
*In the alleys faithless kings.*
          —from "The River"

*Scat singing for the sleep deprived—*
it's what the critics called his
final music, his ship that plowed

some great uncharted dissonance
as if that's where he was headed
all along, to the restless distance

between an ear and its pillow,
between the wind guard of the mike
and insomnia that whispered low

one moment, then rose, cried out
even, leaping five plus octaves,
he would say, though in truth about

two octaves less—still a journey
heavenward and back, a space that grew
wings on his feet, his voice. Joy

became the thread of mercury
in the mouth of a fevered man.
A lie then, the mythical cure

that aged him as he walked bent
high inside the city of angels,
a drop of midnight in his blood.

How he hated the confinement
of old tunes, of the small beach town
that was his bliss. These things he made,

they shadowed him inside the hidden
bungalow he painted black,
the morning nocturne of its curtains.

If no mythology would take him,
there would always be the starless
mandate of the unwritten hymn.

To sail off the edge of the world,
off the end of a spool of tape
where it fluttered on its needle—

tick, tick, tick. Picture a moon
deaf above the sirens of dogs.
It's here where the lost songs begin,

on the brink of a sleep that fears
no less, that closes its eyes to sing,
*Here it comes, at last—no, here. Here.*

# Peal

These long nights the buoy bell shudders
with a weather that blows in fits, compelled,
that swings its giant hammer made of sky
looking to strike a phantom nail, to put
a dent in air only air can mend. To hear it
makes the sleeper turn, though still asleep,
raised half-way like a bucket in a well
to slide back down the buried chamber.
It's the peal of the jagged shoal or just beyond,
the voice that speaks with a mournful
caution, a toll for no one, no one we know,
no ruffle of script on the open page,
only these cold notes of constant warning,
the waves and their steeple that will not drown.
If you hear there the startled timbre
of a clock, it's a drunken one at best,
a clock undone, its troubled stagger sounding
over the vacant spaces, a monster of a clock
grown weary of its size, of the rise
and fall of every hour. What name does time repeat
to death, gone at last illegible, smooth.
And everywhere the music of no musician.
Cry out if you want. It will not hear you.
Only that which never wakes never rests:
the bell's prow and the sea it opens, the chain
it grips, the frightened iron of the sail.

# Djembe

Begin with a goat. I know this much.
To build a djembe you need a goat to match
the rim of the drum. I cannot tell you how

he dies, who's to blame, if he bellows
under the crescent blade, his chafed legs
bound in rope. Whatever legacy

of rope, I cannot say it brings him here,
if his throat calls out in thirst or anger
tethered to its wagon. That ragged scowl

in his sweet face, panicky, skeptical.
Is it any wonder, the ancient heartbreak
of confusion in one who aged too quick.

What is his life but a coin in the red
dust of the morning market. And traded
for what. A coin. That scent on the wind,

that smell of hardening blood, of the wound
we imagine, it's just that: our imagining
something far removed, and yet still singing

in our veins. Begin where tragedies
once began, with the goat-song, the *tragoedie*,
the music, we are told, not of the goat

but of those who would win him, who sing out
at the ritual slaughter of the prize.
Bearded straggler, tough, voracious, wise.

Is there anything he would not eat
as if survival were his god, his art.
Be he African or Greek, what difference.

I want to say he suffers the knife, that he dies
across the threshold of suffering. How else
do we arrive at this, this cargo, these pelts,

this wealth of djembes from the Ivory Coast.
How else the steady flotilla that drums across
the Mid-Atlantic. Begin again, with the best,

the thickest patch of skin, the parched vestment
against the spine, the part the animal
never sees. Take the shock of hide, paled

with sun and mallets, and stretch it; seal it
over a mouth of wood, over the pit
of the departed like a page of stone

now faceless, nameless. Is there no one
at the core of things. Who better to ask,
of all instruments the drum, the oldest,

the first we play terrible as children
in our pens, the first we strike in our frustration
like a door. If only we could open

the shell of that day, its rumored ocean
softly breaking. Each year another child
lost, gone down the darkening spiral

of the ear. Another heaven laid out
against the sacrificial rock of night.
A father's heaven. Begin again, with the end

of one life, how it wants to make children
of us all, and does, children who understand
little of grief's language, of the wind

on their tongues. And so this laying on
of hands, this feral heart we harvest, the one
we hear in the ignorance of rooms, late,

the blood fruit, the hammered gold, the one we let
bloom and die, and bloom, the stubborn one
we chase through the long hollow between

our legs. It's our own warm pulse turned
from distant call to response which in turn
calls out, which knows no future and so

the glad fire of its torch. It's the sound
night makes, just beneath the quiet breathing
of the vents, the flesh exhumed, cut and beating.

# White

And for a time it seemed all music
was the music of my youth,

a pulse I borrowed for my own
strange blood. For a time my dead

friends kept floating to the surface,
their agate eyes wet with sleep.

They have come today, I thought,
to take me out of my body—

expelled or lured, I could not say,
or both, as is the way with songs.

They have come to trouble the water
of each loss, blur it like a harp,

if only to turn me back to see
what the harp sees, what it tells us,

that the world is too full for words,
too empty for them either,

that we live, if we live, in a rented house
under the sound of leaves.

They too are tongues. *Praise,*
said the music, though I remained

a step away, faith on one side,
my shadow on the other, my bones

reinventing themselves again
and again. And for a time day

trailed off like a car radio
gathered deeper into the storm.

The changing sky. It keeps
its promise. This much I know.

*Praise,* said the radio, its song,
its ghost, its bridal veil of rain.

# About Bruce Bond

Bruce Bond's collections of poetry include *Blind Rain* (Finalist, TIL Best Book of Poetry Prize, LSU, 2008), *Cinder* (Finalist, TIL Best Book of Poetry Prize, Etruscan Press, 2003), *The Throats of Narcissus* (University of Arkansas, 2001), *Radiography* (TIL Best Book of Poetry Award, BOA Editions, 1997), *The Anteroom of Paradise* (Colladay Award, QRL, 1991), and *Independence Days* (R. Gross Award, Woodley Press, 1990). His poetry has appeared in *Best American Poetry*, *The Yale Review*, *The Georgia Review*, *Raritan*, *The New Republic*, *The Virginia Quarterly*, *Poetry*, and many other journals. He has received numerous honors including fellowships from the NEA, Texas Commission on the Arts, and other organizations. Presently he is Regents Professor of English at the University of North Texas and Poetry Editor for *American Literary Review*.

# Books from Etruscan Press

Founded in 2001 with a generous grant from the Oristaglio Foundation, Etruscan Press is a non-profit cooperative of poets and writers working to produce and promote books that nurture the dialogue among genres, achieve a distinctive voice, and reshape the literary and cultural histories of which we are a part.

The Etruscan Press publication of the present edition of *Peal* has been made possible by a grant from the
**National Endowment for the Arts.**

NATIONAL
ENDOWMENT
FOR THE ARTS
A great nation
deserves great art.

ETRUSCAN IS PROUD OF SUPPORT RECEIVED FROM

Wilkes University

Youngstown State University

The Wean Foundation

North East Ohio MFA program

The Ohio Arts Council

Council of Literary Magazines and Presses

Nin & James Andrews Foundation

Ruth H. Beecher Foundation

Mary Rhodes

Bates-Manzano Fund

New Mexico Community Foundation

[clmp]

etruscan press
www.etruscanpress.org

Etruscan Press books may be ordered from

Consortium Book Sales and Distribution
800-283-3572
www.cbsd.com

Small Press Distribution
800-869-7553
www.spdbooks.com

Etruscan Press is a 501(c)(3) nonprofit organization.
Contributions to Etruscan Press are tax deductible
as allowed under applicable law.
For more information, a prospectus,
or to order one of our titles,
contact us at etruscanpress@gmail.com.